# Your Father's Business

# Your Father's Business

Letters to a young man about what it means to be a priest from

## Charles W. Harris, c.s.c.

Ave Maria Press
notre dame, indiana 46556

**About the Author**

Rev. Charles W. Harris, C.S.C., is presently engaged in retreat work in Corvallis, Oregon. A graduate of the University of Notre Dame, he received a Master's Degree in Science from the University of Michigan, and did postgraduate work at Yale and the University of Leiden, Holland. He taught physics at the University of Notre Dame, and from 1964 to 1968 he was the Dean of the College of Arts and Sciences at the University of Portland. He served as Associate Newman Chaplain at the University of Michigan during 1968 and 1969, and for seven years, 1969-1976, as a Chaplain at Oregon State University. His previous published works include a *Manual for Antioch Weekends,* a booklet on the Sacrament of Matrimony and numerous articles in religious publications.

With ecclesiastical approval.

© 1978 by Ave Maria Press, Notre Dame, Indiana 46556

Library of Congress Catalog Card Number: 77-93018

International Standard Book Number: 0-87793-146-1

Photography: Jim Hunt: 24, 62.
          Jean-Claude LeJeune: 16, 80.
          Notre Dame Printing & Publications Office:
            cover, 10, 32, 72, 92, 100.
          H. Armstrong Roberts: 40.
          David Strickler: 5, 54, 108.

Printed and bound in the United States of America.

To Bill

# Contents

# Preface

This little book began with a series of letters to Bill, a senior in college, who was trying to make a decision about the priesthood. Several people suggested that they might be helpful for other young men in the same situation. There have been some revisions in the interest of clarity, but the format of the original letters has been retained.

If the intention of these letters had been to influence Bill toward the priesthood, they would deserve an *F,* for Bill and Ann were married in August. Theirs was a decision prayerfully reached and, I think, the right one. I hope these pages may help other young men to hear what the Lord is saying, whether that leads where he has called Bill or where he called me many years ago.

**C.W.H.**

# 1 His Heart Went Out to Them

*"They (Youth) are alone—deeply, tragically alone. They know enough of their materialistic culture . . . to know that it does not work."*

Dear Bill,

After our conversation the other night, when you shared that you had been thinking about the priesthood and the possibility of breaking up with Ann, I felt a real joy in my heart. Not at the thought of breaking up with Ann, of course. I told you when you first started going with her that there was no one whom I would rather see you interested in. But you have so many natural abilities that fit you for the priesthood, and the Lord has been giving you so many graces, that this may be what he is preparing you for. Then, today, as I was thinking about what we had said, there came to my mind the words: "When Jesus disembarked he saw the large crowd and his heart went out to them because they were as sheep without a shepherd."

A lot of thoughts filled my mind. Later I developed them for the guys and girls in our prayer group and, although this may be a bit formal for a letter, I want to share them with you.

The apostles had been so busy with people coming and going that they had not even time for meals. And so Jesus said, "Come alone by yourselves to some quiet place and rest a little." But the crowd saw them leave in the boat and followed them along the shore. Jesus and his disciples had only begun to rest when the crowd caught up with them, breathless from their haste, dirty from the sand of the shore and hungering for more words from Jesus. And so, tired as he was, he sat down to teach them for the rest of the day. And they listened, for here was one who understood the emptiness of their lives and the longing in their hearts. As evening came on, he felt hungry and he knew they were, so he multiplied the loaves and the fishes that they might be refreshed.

"His heart went out to them because they were as sheep without a shepherd."

A young college student recently told me of a combination pot and beer party he had engaged in with some of his friends—how the conversation had come around to the problem of God and the meaninglessness of life. Go to the limit in being spaced out, indulge every pleasurable sensation to the hilt; life is a squirrel cage. When you have exhausted its possibilities, jump off.

"And his heart went out to them because they were as sheep without a shepherd."

You see them everywhere with backpacks, hitching along the highway, alone or in couples. They are dropouts from school, runaways from home, experimenting with sex, tasting its pleasure but not its commitment. They seek in casual encounters the love they are longing for but have never experienced, trying through drugs to experience a world beyond their senses, a world that their deepest instincts tell them exists, but which they have never known.

They are alone—deeply, tragically alone. They know enough of their materialistic culture and civilization to know that it does not satisfy. "Man does not live by bread alone," but there is no one to break with them the Bread of Life.

"And his heart went out to them because they were as sheep without a shepherd."

She was not a good woman, as reputations go, and even less of a housekeeper, and so it was past noon before she came with her bucket to the well. There in the shade sat a Jew, weariness etched in the lines in his face and the shadows under his eyes. Tired though he was, he entered into conversation with her, asked her for a drink, told her she had had five husbands and the man she was living with now was not her husband. He took time for her, stirred in her heart such a mixture of sorrow and joy that she rushed into the city saying, "Come and see a man who has told me everything I ever did. Could this be the Messiah?"

How many there were like her who only needed someone to take time with them, love them enough to show them where they were wrong, tell them how much God longs to fill the emptiness of their lives.

As Jesus sat there looking over the land, he said to his disciples, "Look around on the fields. They are ripe, ready for harvest." God has prepared their hearts; they are ready to believe.

But how can they have faith in one they have never heard of? And how hear without someone to spread the news? How could anyone spread the news without a commission to do so, as the scripture affirms, "How welcome are the feet of the messengers of good news" (Rom 10:13).

God does not desert his people. "His

heart goes out to them because they are as sheep without a shepherd."

Jesus of Nazareth walked along the seashore among the fishermen he had known and he said, "Come, follow me." It was an absolute call and not all accepted it. One wanted to wait until his old father had died, another wanted to visit his farm, a third was just married and therefore could not come, another turned away sad for he had great possessions. Some followed, like Peter and the eleven and said, "We have left all that we ever had" — home, wife, brothers, parents, children — "and followed you." They had left them all for the sake of the kingdom of God. "You have not chosen me," Jesus said, "I have chosen you."

And then, before he returned to the Father, he entrusted to them his lambs, his sheep, his big sheep, because to the question, "Do you love me more than all things else?" came the reply, "Master, you know all things. You know that I love you." They had answered the call, they had accepted the commission to bring the good news to the end of the world. Was it hard? Of course, it was hard, for these are men of flesh and blood, men of great warmth and great capacity to love, who left parents, wives, brothers, sisters, children.

Today there are 48,881,872 Catholics in the United States. There are 58,847 priests

counting all who breathe. If one discounts those who are retired, those engaged in non-pastoral work, there is slightly less than one priest for every thousand Catholics. That might be adequate if there were detailed pastoral planning, but there isn't; if there were a division of ministries and the whole Christian body was exercising those ministries effectively and responsibly, but that is not taking place. Half of these priests are 50 or over. In another ten years, for all practical purposes, 29,000 of those priests will not be functioning or they will be doing so in a very limited capacity. There are 17,000 students in seminaries. One cannot anticipate more than 12,000 being ordained. There will be 17,000 less priests to minister to 48 million Catholics ten years from now, assuming the Church does not grow.

"When Jesus saw the large crowd, his heart went out to them because they were as sheep without a shepherd."

In a recent survey of Catholic opinion, 73 percent of Catholics approve of remarriage after divorce, 72 percent would allow for the abortion of a malformed fetus, 83 percent sanction artificial contraception in spite of the very clear teaching of the bible and tradition on the first two. Only 50 percent attend Mass regularly. Clearly, the people are confused, like sheep without shepherds. And one must be quite frank and say that some of the shepherds have been confused as well.

At the Ascension, Jesus left his work in the hands of men. By the very fact that the Son of God became man, man had been raised up, touched with divinity, made apt to carry on the work of Jesus Christ. "One man would plant, another would water, it is true, but God would give the increase."

The whole increase is, indeed, the work of God but there is no increase unless there is one who plants—the apostle—and one who waters—the pastor. It is no less true today that Jesus is again saying, "Follow me." He is still deeply concerned for those who are like sheep without a shepherd. The harvest is great but the laborers are few—and his invitation is being rejected. To give oneself totally and unreservedly to the kingdom is always an invitation that can be refused or accepted.

Today there are 20,000 less sisters in the U.S. than in 1956 and schools and orphanages and hospitals have closed because there is a decreasing interest in feeding the hungry, visiting the sick, clothing the naked. These statistics, analyzed any way you want, do not point to a vigorous Church.

By contrast, in these same 20 years, Mother Teresa, a wisp of a nun, has gathered about her 5,000 nuns, largely from Asia and Africa, to do this work.

The major objection that is raised today about the priesthood is the problem of celibacy. Let me say right off that this generation has been oversold on sex and the idea that one cannot be a completely fulfilled individual without a sexual relationship. For Christians, this gets translated to mean no one can be completely fulfilled "without marriage." As Graham Pulkingham has stated so well, the only thing you have when an incomplete person gets married is an incomplete married person.

History indicates that esteem for marriage goes hand in hand with esteem for the dedicated, single life. "Each has his proper gift," Paul says, and when the dedicated, single life is no longer regarded as a gift of the Spirit, neither is marriage.

The great problem of celibacy is not sexuality but loneliness, and I must say that in all my celibate life I have never known as much loneliness as have some married people I know. There is little remedy for loneliness in sharing your bed but not your heart. Conversely, celibacy is not possible, ordinarily, without the loving support of a Christian community. Every Christian community should really consider itself lacking in the full expression of the gospel if it does not have dedicated single people living a life of celibacy in its midst.

To appreciate, love and esteem the celibate life takes nothing away from the appreciation, love and esteem of marriage. God in his mysterious providence calls some to one, others to the other. When the wisdom of God and his loving providence for his people are reverenced, then each of his invitations is met with wonder, respect and love.

God calls the whole Christian community to the work of sharing the good news, but long ago Paul made clear that part-time workers are not sufficient, that there must be men and women totally given to the work of the kingdom if the efforts of the others are to be fruitful and effective. He writes, "The unmarried man is free to concern himself with the Lord's affairs, and how he may please him. But the married man is sure to be concerned also with matters of this world, that he may please his wife—his interests are divided." Paul was not saying this to cut down marriage. He was pointing out a very practical difficulty that is a consequence and responsibility of marriage and he was saying that there must be some with an undivided interest in the work of the kingdom.

Catherine Doherty writes in *The Gospel Without Compromise,* "The agony of the

Church is in my bones these days. Long are the nights, the sleepless nights that grip me and will not let me go . . . youth is seeking after new and old ways of prayer. They are turning toward the building of communities and communes."

Yes, the fields are ripe and ready for the harvest. Jesus saw them and his heart went out to them because they were as sheep without shepherds.

Where are the shepherds?
Where are those whose hearts will go out?
Where are those who will gather the harvest?
Pray the Lord of the harvest that he send laborers into his harvest.

I don't want to pressure you into a decision. I am sharing these thoughts because there is a real need. "God Needs Men" was the title of a movie years ago. And it's true. Each of us has the power to short-circuit the Incarnation and Redemption when we fail to respond to what God wants to do in our lives. Just be open to the possibility that God is calling you to be a priest. I know you are afraid of that.

If he is really calling you, there will begin to be an attraction to this life, an attraction which becomes stronger and clearer when you are peaceful and your heart is at rest, most especially when these moments are moments of prayer. This is one thing that you and only you can discern. It must be a discernment in the sense that you *know* that the Lord is saying, "Come," and you are ready to say, "Yes," or at least that you are pretty sure that is what he is saying.

A lot of side issues can obscure the fundamental decision, like what you have to give up, what you have to gain. There should be no sense of compulsion, for instance, of having to do something that basically you hate to do. What you want to do is freely to say "Yes" to a basic attraction, even though that "Yes" may involve some real pain as a consequence.

No, I don't think you should break up with Ann, at least not for now. But put your relationship on the back burner, so to speak. You can get so emotionally involved in a relationship that it is almost impossible to make an objective decision. You are going to be apart for the summer. That will help you sort things out calmly and peacefully.

Perhaps, during the summer when I have more time, I can share some other thoughts on the priesthood that will help in your decision.

Spending a few days at the Trappists is a good idea. I will be praying and fasting for you while you are there.

May the God of peace make you holy through and through. He who calls you is utterly faithful and will finish what he has set out to do in you.

**In His love,**
**C.W.H.**

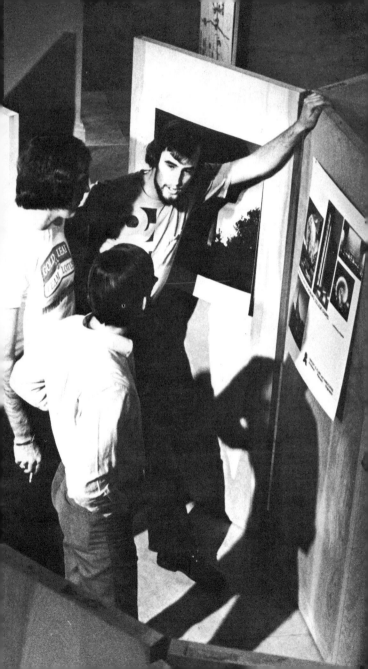

# 2 I Will Make You Fishers of Men

*"As we move from a highly clerical institution to something that more nearly approaches the people of God . . . what does a priest do?"*

Dear Bill,

In my last letter, I said I hoped to find time to share some thoughts about the priesthood with you. Now I think this is important enough to *make* time for it.

Today the Church is rediscovering and renewing a whole variety of ministries. You've seen this from our work together in the campus ministry. You've talked to students and older people and even priests and sisters about prayer, about the humanness of Jesus — traditionally something only a priest might have done. And you have found joy and satisfaction in doing that.

Priesthood is not necessary to do a lot of things priests have done, and that makes a decision about the priesthood all the harder. But this development of ministries begins to make real the statement, "We are the Church."

As we move from a highly clerical institution to something that more nearly approaches the people of God as described in Vatican II, the question arises, what does the priest do? Or, what is left for the priest to do?

So I want to indicate something of the services to the Christian community that can be given only by the priest as distinguished from services that don't require a permanent commission. Then, at the end, I will pose some practical remarks that will help you discern what the Lord wants of you.

What is asked of the Christian is total commitment, the total living out, at each moment, that "Jesus is Lord." What is asked of the priest, in addition, is total service to the Christian community. It is to lay down one's life for one's brother, not in a single burst of generosity like the love of the martyrs which bursts into crimson glory in the actual handing over of life, but to place one's whole life at the disposal of others every day. That's what the call of the apostles means.

"Jesus said, 'Come and follow me, and I will teach you to catch men.' At once they dropped their nets and followed him. Then he went a little farther along the shore and saw James, the son of Zebedee, aboard a boat with his brother John, overhauling their nets. At once he called them, and they left their father Zebedee in the boat with the hired men, and went off after him" (Mt 1:17-20).

The call to follow Jesus is the call given to all Christians. The call given to follow him and to become fishers of men is the call given to the apostle, the call given to the priest. The apostles are not the only ones to follow Jesus. There are great crowds who listen to him. Among them are people he rebukes for not taking care of their parents (Mk 7:9-14). One of the things he said to the rich young man who wanted to possess eternal life was to keep the commandments—honor (care for) your father and mother, etc.

But of the apostle he requires that he leave father, mother, wife, children, lands, for the sake of the kingdom or, as we would say today, for the sake of the Christian community. That kind of leaving Jesus does not ask of everyone who follows him. That kind of leaving can only be required for the sake of the kingdom.

In John, Chapter 10, Jesus says, "I am the Good Shepherd." Actually, the Greek says the ideal shepherd, the one upon whom all shepherds (pastor is the Latin word for shepherd) must be patterned. "The good shepherd will give his life for the sake of his sheep." Notice the totality of the commitment to the flock. And if one recalls the shepherd of Palestine in the time of Jesus, the understanding is even more clear. For that shepherd very literally left home and lived with the sheep for months, moving with them to wherever green pasture could be found.

"I am the Good Shepherd and I know my own and my own know me, just as the Father knows me and I know the Father." The comparison really breaks down a bit here, for now it is a knowledge of the sheep by the shepherd, a knowledge of the shepherd by the sheep, that can only be compared to the total knowledge, total sharing, total love of the Father and the Son.

Do you remember when we were at Don and Marcia's during the spring break how the sheep recognized Don's voice and followed him when he came to let them out into the field? But they didn't recognize you and ran away. That old ewe got mighty upset when you picked up one of her lambs. (You were lucky the ram wasn't around.) The sheep knew the shepherd and so, too, "The real shepherd knows his sheep by name."

"The real shepherd knows his sheep by

name." In the gospel the "name" is not a handle for identification. It means the totality of the person, that which is most intimate to and distinctive of the person. Jesus knows all that, knows it as he knows the Father, knows the weakness and the strength, the struggle and the ability, the failure and success of each of the flock.

At the end of the Gospel of John, Jesus makes it clear that those whom he called to be fishers of men have to be this kind of shepherd. In John 21 we come across the same crowd he first called, including Peter and the sons of Zebedee, who are going fishing again. They catch nothing all night, even until morning, when Jesus calls to them from the shore. He tells them where to cast their nets, and they have the best day of fishing in their fishing careers. Then he cooks their breakfast and after breakfast he says to Peter, "Simon, son of John, do you love me more than these?"

"Yes, Lord," he replied. "You know that I love you."

"Then feed my lambs," replied Jesus.

Three times Jesus does this, and each time he gives a portion of the flock until all is handed over to Peter. It is very clear that he is designating Peter to take his place as shepherd. Peter is the chief shepherd, he has care of the whole flock, the others care for part of the flock. They are to be shepherds like he has been.

To everyone he calls to the priesthood, Jesus puts the same question, "Do you love me more than these?" It is not quite clear what "these" refers to, but most commentators say the sense of the question is, "Do you love me more than anything else?" This I think is really the heart of the question: Do you love me so totally and so completely that I can trust you with these sheep whom I loved so much that I gave my life for them? Are you so filled with love for me that my love for them can be poured out through you? Do you love them enough to give your life? Do you love me enough to give your life for them? And when Peter had said, "Lord, you know everything. You know that I love you," Jesus told him that, like him, Peter would give his earthly life. That is what it means to be a real shepherd, a real priest—each day to give one's life for his sheep. That is why Bishop Sheen emphasizes so much the priest-victim.

Today we often make the mistake of identifying the priesthood with celibacy: priesthood = celibacy. I think celibacy is a consequence of being a priest, but one will fail to understand priesthood if one thinks of it simply in terms of celibacy. Monks and hermits are celibates although they are not usually priests. Nuns are celibate and are not priests. There is an increasing number of people who are living celibate lives in Christian communities and working in the world. Celibacy is not priesthood. Celibacy is a consequence of being willing to lay down one's life for the flock.

When Jesus asked Peter if he loved him, he was asking for a very special kind of love. It was a love of choice, a love of friendship that wants to share all things. At the Last Supper, Jesus said, "I no longer call you my students but my friends, because I have shared with you all that I have heard from my Father."

Are they willing to share everything with him? the Lord asks. Friendship is a two-way street. There is a special love between Jesus and the priest because of the depth and extent of the sharing. We know the quality of our friendships depends on the depth and extent of our sharing. Our friendship with one is not the same as with another because different things are shared. Here I am not saying that the priest loves Jesus more than anybody else or that Jesus loves the priest more than anyone else. But there is a special kind of love here.

As a priest you share in a knowledge of the flock in a way that only Jesus shares —

"I know mine and mine know me." For, as a priest, people open their hearts to you. You know the burden of sin in their lives and how it is hurting them, pressing them down, warping them, and you love them with the love of Jesus and you suffer with him because of what sin is doing, and there is only one person in all the world you can share this knowledge with, this suffering with, and that is Jesus Christ. Quoist really puts it very well in the "Prayer of a Priest on Sunday Night":

It's hard to suffer from the sins of others, and yet be obliged to hear and bear them

It's hard to be told secrets, and be unable to share them

It's hard to carry others and never, even for a moment, to be carried

It's hard to be alone, alone before suffering, death, sin. . . .

Son, you are not alone, I am with you, I am you. Out of all eternity I chose you, I need you.

(From *Prayers,*
Sheed Andrews and McMeel)

As a priest you come to know the hidden beauty of men's lives and hearts and you are filled with great joy at this beauty and the way they grow. Most of the time there is only one person with whom you can share this joy and that is Jesus Christ. Because you share these things with him, there is a special love, a special friendship.

And the Lord gives himself to you, trusts himself to you. After 34 years, I still cannot say Mass without a sense of unreality. Is it really I who can make Jesus Christ present on the altar? That where he will be, where he will gather his people into his complete and total offering to the Father, is dependent on me? His love, his abiding with his people, his forgiveness are put into my hands—my very, very human hands—to pour out on his people permanently and unfailingly. "Whose sins you shall forgive, they are forgiven."

The charismatic gifts of the Spirit are poured out on each member of the community for the building up of the whole. Yet the greater part of these gifts is not possessed in a permanent way. They come into being only through the impulse of the Spirit. The gift of prophecy, the gift of healing, the wisdom gifts are transitory. They cannot be exercised when I will. Their exercise is completely dependent upon the Spirit. That is their glory, for the power of the Spirit is thereby manifested, but it is also their handicap. Jesus gives to the priest permanent powers because the priest is permanently and totally given to the service of the

Christian community. "I am with you all days."

When the priest anoints the sick, the healing power of Jesus operates through him. When the priest pronounces forgiveness of sin, touches the heart with inner healing, Jesus is forgiving and healing. When the priest says, "This is my body," it is the body of Jesus. The action of Jesus is identified with the action of the priest always, unvaryingly, inevitably. The power of Jesus operates through the priest in a permanent way because he is in the total and permanent service of the Christian community. That is what he is called to. That is what he is consecrated to. That is his life.

While each Christian has a gift and a service, the gift is transitory and the service part-time. Essential to the priest is total service, permanent dedication to the community.

In the Letter to the Hebrews it says: "Every high priest is (1) taken from among men and (2) appointed their representative before God (3) to offer gifts and sacrifices for sins. (4) He is able to bear patiently with the ignorant and erring since he, too, is beset by weakness . . . no one takes this to himself but only he who is called by God."

(1) "Taken from among men" — above all things, he should be normal. He should have a healthy interest in girls, a natural desire for marriage and the friendship of a woman, a love for children, an emotional balance. You would really qualify on this point.

(2) He is to go to God for men. He is to be chosen, therefore, by God. No man is worthy, nor can he be. God distributes his gifts as he will. No man is called to be a priest because of his virtue. No man is a priest for himself. He is a priest for others. He is to minister to and build up the body.

(3) He must be deeply aware of his own sinfulness that he may have compassion on weakness. His heart "must go out to them for they are as sheep without shepherds." He must have a growing willingness to be a victim—to give his life that others may live.

How does one know that God is calling him?

(1) By one's gifts and abilities. Many of these are necessary for any occupation, but as all, or almost all, begin to converge in an individual, there is serious reason to consider whether God is calling that person to the priesthood. Perhaps I can indicate some of these by a series of questions.

(a) Is the Lord giving me gifts or has he

given me gifts that will serve many, in contrast to the gifts given to a husband and father who will serve a few?

(b) Is the Lord giving me the ability to approach many people of varying personalities and to share him with them?

(c) Is he giving me the ability to talk effectively to *groups* of people and to bring to them the message of Jesus?

(d) Is there a growing concern for all people, the desire to touch and to heal the wounds of their hearts?

(2) There is a growing conviction that the Lord is saying, "Come, follow me, and I will make you a fisher of men." This may take the form of a growing desire for a life of total service to the Christian community, in contrast to the part-time service of a member of the community. There is a sense that God is calling me to be a permanent instrument of his ministry.

(3) Sometimes this conviction meets with eagerness. First, one sort of entertains the idea. Then, "Lord, if that is what you want, I am ready." Finally, *leaving all* things I follow him. At other times one hears and tries to shut out the sound of the Lord's voice. Deep down, we know that it is the Lord. He is

saying, "Go, sell everything . . . and come, follow me." At times there is a very active rebellion—Why me, Lord? Look, I'm graduating, I've got a job, I've got a girl, everything I want out of life. Why me?

(4) If the thought of the priesthood makes one angry, rebellious, or abnormally fearful, one can suspect the Lord is calling. We don't ordinarily react strongly to something that has no particular meaning for us.

If one has the interior disposition to follow the Lord no matter where he calls and no matter what has to be given up, then if one is leading a life of prayer—daily, on a regular basis, giving the Lord time to get at him—what God wants will become clear. The conviction grows stronger and stronger; the rebellion, the fear, the anger quiet down. An inner peace and the assuring voice of the Lord come. "My grace is sufficient for you." So many people think that if God calls someone to the priesthood it is a call to misery. God never calls to misery. He may call to sacrifice; he never calls to unhappiness. It is safe to put our lives in his hands, no matter what he asks, for he loves us better than we love ourselves.

You have probably already realized from the excess postage that this letter is to be read on the installment plan. Sorry to be so windy but I just had a lot to put in focus.

"There is a great deal more I want to say to you but I can't put it down in black and white. I hope to see you before long, and we will have a heart-to-heart talk. Peace be with you" (3 Jn).

**In His love,
C.W.H.**

P.S. I'm going to Madras for Bob and Sally's wedding. I'll pack a lunch and stop off at the farm to see you and the paint job you are giving the place.

# 3 Stay Here and Watch With Me

*"In a certain sense the priest is rootless and so is at the disposal of the needs of the Gospel."*

Dear Bill,

Bob and Chris came over Saturday to begin their marriage instructions while I was close by in Medford. Several times I made some allusions to the date of the wedding and got only vague responses. Finally, came the dawn and I turned to Bob with the question, "Bob, have you ever asked Chris to marry you?"

Unromantic Bob replied, "Well, we've talked about it but I guess I never really have." So I said, "Don't you think you ought to ask her before we go any further?" So Bob turns to Chris and says, "Chris, will you marry me?" and she said, "Yes."

That sort of blew my mind. Bob said, "Charlie, I'll bet that's the first time you have ever been in on a proposal." And it was. Then he said, "Wait a minute," went out to the car and came back with a ring he had been carrying around for a suitable time to give Chris. So I blessed it and he slipped it on her finger. Fortunately I had a bottle of wine in the refrigerator so the event did not go uncelebrated. Only Bob could get away with something like that.

In my last letter I said that what is distinctive about the priest is not total commitment to Jesus Christ, for that is characteristic of all Christians, but total commitment to the Christian community.

It is not always easy to distinguish in the gospels the call of Jesus to be a Christian, "Follow me," from his call to be an apostle, "Follow me, and I will make you fishers of men." Sometimes it seems that the two calls coincide. Nevertheless, the gospels make it clear that when Jesus chooses his apostles he chooses them from among his disciples, i.e., from those who have been following him. Mark 3:14 and Matthew 10:1 tell us that he appointed twelve:

    (1)  to be with him

    (2)  to be sent out to preach

(3)  to have authority to cast out demons

(4)  to heal every disease and infirmity.

Sometimes we just zip through the gospel phrases and miss the reality they put so briefly. I want to recreate that reality if I can. This is not an excerpt from one of my scripture classes but it may sound like it.

### *To Be with Him*

They traveled together, they ate together, they shared the same earth in sleep. They are taught by him and the gospels make clear that the twelve alone receive the fullness of his teaching. They alone share that dreadful moment of weakness that lay hold on him when "he began to be horror-stricken and desperately depressed. 'My heart is nearly breaking,' he said to them. 'Stay here and keep watch with me.'"

It takes great openness and great trust to share one's weakness, but at this moment he could, for "he had made it that they should be always with him." John 13 makes clear that being with him is much more than simply sharing his company. They are to be profoundly associated with him in his suffering, in his death.

When he lays aside his outer garment and puts on the garment of a slave (because he is to do the work of a slave) and washes their feet, Peter is the one who finally recovers enough from the shock to say, "Lord, you will never wash my feet."

Perhaps he is the last to have his feet washed, perhaps he is the one who has the clearest vision of who Jesus is. Certainly, the gospels show him to us as a man who oscillates between the clarity of his faith-vision and his weakness.

With a faith in no way as clear or as strong as his, I would certainly have said, "Lord, you will never wash my feet." And Jesus says to Peter, "If I do not wash your feet you will have no part in me." The washing of the feet is something much more than a gesture of service. Without it, he will not have part with Jesus.

To understand the incident fully we need to remember that at the Last Supper only the twelve are gathered. The part which they are to have in Jesus is distinctive of them as twelve. The washing of the feet symbolizes the Passion which purifies the world and it is the symbol of the intimate association in his redeeming work to which they are called. Washing the feet is the work of a slave and he is, indeed, the Suffering Servant or slave of Isaiah 53:

Yet on himself he bore our sufferings
    our torments he endured
                . . .

He was pierced for our transgressions,
   tortured for our iniquities;
The chastisement he bore is health for us
   and by his scourging we are healed.
We had all strayed like sheep,
   each of us had gone his own way,
But the Lord laid upon him the guilt of us
   all.

How they are to be associated with him is
made clear in another action at the Last
Supper: "On the night he was betrayed he
took bread and when he had given thanks, he
broke it and said, 'This is my body which is
given for you. *Do this in memory of me.*' "

They were to be associated with him in
his suffering redemption because it would be
through them "that the body broken, the
blood poured out" would be presented to his
people in every time. This would remind them
of a love so great that he gave his life for his
friends, of a prodigal generosity that spent
life "that we might have life and have it more
abundantly."

It would be the reminder, not of a simple
word, but of a creative and redeeming word
that makes actually present him who bears
the marks of the nails forever. To each of us,
as to the doubting Thomas, he is made
present as the eternal victim and says, "Put
your finger here, and touch my hands, and put
out your hand and place it in my side; do not
be faithless but believing."

Faith comes through contact with the risen Jesus and it is in the Eucharist and all that leads to it that we touch the human risenness of Jesus and are made whole in faith and heart. To be the instrument of this saving faith is "to have part in him."

"When he had washed their feet and put on his garments . . . he said to them, 'If I, your lord and master, have washed your feet, then you also ought to wash one another's feet.' "

"Do this in memory of me."

He reminded them that their association with him made them servants or slaves to their brothers and that through their service others were to have part with him. For the priest is the instrument by which Calvary is made present for everyone at each moment of time.

The priest, too, is called to be victim. His role is with the suffering Jesus, as well as with the risen Jesus. He is to be a victim in no self-pitying way, but always in that self-forgetting generosity of washing his brothers' feet. As the plaque in our kitchen—above the sink, Roger's contribution—put it: "Whose feet will you wash if you live alone?" The priest can never be a man for himself alone. The priest's is a life with no rights, except the great right to serve . . . even when he knows that he is serving badly. For he knows that he is an unprofitable servant, a servant who can never love and serve as his Master has done.

### *He Is Sent Out to Preach*

It would be much better to translate this "to proclaim" for he comes as the bringer of good news, the bearer of joy. It would be foolish to deny, even if one wanted to, that every Christian is called to preach the gospel where he is. But that which characterizes the preaching of the apostle—the priest—is that he is sent out. In a certain sense he is rootless and so is at the disposal of the needs of the gospel.

There is a freedom about him "to be sent" to wherever the gospel needs to be preached. He is not tied down. He can be a man on the move. That is why Jesus can instruct the apostles to go out and "to take nothing beyond a walking-stick, no bread, no pack, no money in their belts" Mk 6:9.

Secondly, in a particular way the apostles speak for him—"He who hears you hears me; he who despises you despises me." There is a ministry of the word which is unique to the priesthood. As Paul says, "You may have many teachers; you have but one Father." The tradition of the Church, the sacrament of Holy Orders, indicates a particular commis-

47

sion and a special grace of announcing the word. It is not surprising, therefore, that for the priest living in close union with Jesus Christ there is a particular effectiveness to his ministry of the word.

### To Have Authority to Cast Out Demons

When the apostles are sent out it is to share in the work of Jesus and that means to put an end to the dominion of Satan over men's lives. "Lord," they said, "evil spirits obey us when we use your name." All Christians are so commissioned and so empowered. But after the Resurrection, Jesus imparts to the apostles a particular power over Satan that is peculiar to them as apostles. "He said to them: 'Just as the Father sent me, so I am going to send you' (we recall that an apostle is one who is sent). And then he breathed upon them and said, 'Receive the Holy Spirit. If you forgive any man's sins, they are forgiven, and if you hold them unforgiven, they are unforgiven.' "

The power of Satan is very real and leads to slavery. The power of forgiveness is the power to set free. As Karl Rahner puts it: "Despite his membership in the people of God and the body of Christ, the Christian is prey to temptations from within and without. The danger is that, yielding, he will establish a system of values in which it is no longer

God that stands at the center of his willing and thinking but a creature, whether a person or a thing . . ."

Paul says (Romans), "You are slaves of the power which you choose to obey, whether you choose sin, whose reward is death, or God, obedience to whom means the reward of righteousness."

Our Christian life is not a straight progression upwards. Baptism leads us into a new life, but it is still the life of a baby Christian, subject to many influences which may weaken or destroy it. Satan may be repulsed by one effort, but he is never destroyed by it. He returns again and again, and sometimes we Christians yield. And so the sacrament of Reconciliation is given that the Christian may be aided in shaking off the slavery of Satan to whom he has become subject and make welcome him who is rightful Lord. True freedom consists in obedience to him.

When we fail we need not only the encouragement of fellow Christians to rise above our failure, but also to have spoken to us the word of God. More powerful than any sword, the word cuts with one  stroke the chains that bind us. It is not enough for us to say to the Lord, "I'm sorry. Forgive me." Our humanness wants to hear his word spoken to us, "I forgive you." When that word is spoken, our hearts are filled with peace, as when Jesus commanded the angry waves to be still and they were. The word "Satan" means the accuser and he stands there accusing when we have asked for forgiveness (cf. Rv 12:10-12). Nothing silences him quite so effectively as the reconciling words of the sacrament of Reconciliation, "In the name of Jesus Christ I forgive you."

Here, too, in the sacrament of Reconciliation, inner healing is effected. One can help people understand the root of their sinfulness, the inner hurts carried around for a long time against which they are still reacting—the lack of appreciation, the lack of encouragement, the resentments at being put down. As you pray with them and speak God's sacramental word you know that healing is taking place.

To be God's instrument in this reconciliation is a supreme joy. I remember hearing confessions from 7:30 until 11:00 on Christmas Eve when I was at Yale. There was a lull, so I looked out of the confessional. The church was empty except for one man and I waited and waited for him—with increasing impatience. Slowly, I heard his footsteps approaching the confessional. "Bless me, Father, for I have sinned. It has been 25 years since my last confession." To see Christ born again in the life of this man filled me with inexpressible joy. I could not be grateful enough to God for making me a priest.

### *To Heal Every Disease and Infirmity*

Again, each Christian is called to minister healing and God gives a special gift to some. In a particular way the healing power of Jesus is entrusted to the priest as minister of the Anointing of the Sick. It is good to reflect that this ministry is to "every disease and infirmity," and not simply to those character- ized by bodily ailment.

It is estimated that 80 percent of our physical illnesses have their origin in mental or emotional disorder. Like the woman in the gospel, therefore, the beginning of the physical healing may be to reach out and to touch Jesus, or rather to reach out to him who is already reaching out to us. An awful lot of physical healing must begin by healing of the spirit. That is why the Anointing of the Sick is often so effective. I have never administered the sacrament without seeing an improvement within 24 hours.

Yesterday (Tuesday) I was called to the hospital, to the Intensive Care Unit. A young man on a motorcycle had run into a bridge abutment while rounding a sharp corner. He was not responding and the nurse said death was a matter of only a few hours. He was unconscious, and while I prayed with him and for him, I knew I could not reach him. Then I anointed him and his head stirred and I thought he might be coming to consciousness.

Perhaps at that moment he did, and accepted the presence of Jesus in the sacrament. I had a real sense of joy at knowing the Lord could reach where I could not. That night I went to Sally's for the prayer meeting. She had invited a number of Catholics who had no experience of the charismatic renewal for an introductory talk and Mass. I had intended to offer the Mass for someone in the parish, but as I began the Canon the Lord said, "Offer it for Ralph."

I thought Ralph must be dead by now and I would offer Mass for him on Sunday when I had a free intention. As I moved to the Consecration, I was having a real struggle—when you are saying Mass you can't stop to discern whether something is from the Lord or yourself—but the impulse was very forceful and so I stopped for a moment and said, "O.K., Lord, I offer this Mass for Ralph." The next day I found out that Ralph had not died until Wednesday morning. Perhaps I shall never know this side of eternity why that word from the Lord came, but somehow it was something Ralph needed to push him into the arms of the Lord.

Being a priest is not easy. You want love and intimacy and friendship. Sometimes you find a warm and loving Christian community which supports you and meets those needs. Sometimes you don't and you are very much alone. But I have no regrets after 34 years, and no matter what the cost I would never want to have been anything else.

This is the heaviest bit I shall lay on you. But I wanted to give you some insight into what being a priest means, both in ideal and in reality. Of course, like marriage, you never really know until you are in it. As Aristotle put it: "It is necessary to think a long time when you can decide but once."

I hope your pinochle game is improving. I'm getting bored with so many victories and the lack of competition. Why don't you go over to Tim and Mary Jo's for a lesson or two?

God's peace! It's one a.m. and the morning is too closely joined to the night.

**In His love,
C.W.H.**

# 4 Ministers of a New Covenant

*"We need to dream and plan new forms of Christian community that meet our needs. . . . Without the community the priest has no function."*

Dear Bill,

I really appreciated your call this morning and I'll check with AAA about scenic spots on the way to Ohio. I should like to stop at Yellowstone and the Craters of the Moon and, in general, make the trip a leisurely one. Steve is going to give the car a tune-up and check the tires.

You asked how I decided to become a priest and whether I had gone through all the questioning you are. Briefly, no! Mine was a different time and situation, but calling it to mind might not be totally out of place.

Much of my growing up was on a farm in

Indiana and our nearest neighbors were a half-mile away. We saw a lot of the neighbors in summertime, for they pitched in to help one another with the haying or cooking the mint stills. We had a telephone and were on a party line and if you got tremendously bored, you could always listen in on a telephone conversation—if your mother wasn't around.

Eventually, we got an Atwater-Kent radio which ran on batteries—when it ran. It had more dials to adjust than a 707, and if you were fortunate and got them all set just right, you might occasionally pick up a voice from Chicago around midnight. But the distortion was so great, the static so loud, and the squealing so shrill that you couldn't make anything out, except perhaps the station identification.

Every morning we took the bus at eight o'clock, four and a half miles to the parochial school. At 8:30 we formed ranks under the guidance of the sisters and marched in silence to Mass where we said the confiteor together in English and the offertory prayers. The rest of the time one of the eighth-graders led the rosary. After school we had 15 minutes to catch the bus for home. There were always chores to be done and, after supper, lessons by the Coleman lantern and the kitchen stove. Once in a while we would stay for a movie at school which cost a nickel. We saw some of Charlie Chaplin and a lot of Our Gang comedies.

We drove to the 10 a.m. Mass on Sunday and that usually lasted one and a half hours and then came home and had a big dinner. After I got my gun, I used to go hunting in the afternoon. Saturday was always a workday, except in winter. I acquired a taste for reading and every week brought home three books from the public library. My mother, who was well-read, always checked the books over first and from time to time would say, "You can read this one when you are a little older."

In the sixth grade I read *David Copperfield* and *Vanity Fair* and enjoyed them both. By now I was getting book lists from school of approved books. My mother would read them with me and we would talk about them. Many nights we said the rosary and always during Lent and Advent and October, which seemed most of the year.

My mother had what we called the Doctor's Book which she would consult for symptoms and remedies for childhood diseases. The doctor came only when a baby came, and the whole proceeding was surrounded by a great deal of mystery, and I never knew where babies came from until I was in the sixth grade. Then one Saturday afternoon in winter, when my mother was gone, I got into the Doctor's Book and discovered sex. We had seen the animals born but had never put two and two together.

In the sixth grade we also heard about the Sixth Commandment and dirty thoughts. I sort of figured that's what I had when I read the Doctor's Book and I had better tell it in confession. So I did. The priest was an old German who gave me a terrific going-over. I was going to hell if I kept that up. We used to go to confession on Friday afternoon— school was out an hour early. My sister said, "You were in there a long time. I'm going to tell Mom." I gave her my pocketknife so she wouldn't and it's the only time she didn't tell my mother everything she knew—about me. After that I decided to keep my bad thoughts to myself and never tell them in confession again, if the priest got so upset.

About the only time I was away from home was each summer when I got to visit my aunt and uncle for two weeks. My cousin, Ben, was two years older than I and used words like "damn" and "shit" which he had learned from working with the farmhands on the onion farm. I used them once when I got home and got my mouth washed out with soap. My aunt and uncle lived in town in a great big house and owned a farm besides. I thought they were very rich and Ben and I got to go to the movies on Saturday afternoon. I saw

Douglas Fairbanks and Mary Pickford in *Robin Hood* and promptly fell in love with Mary Pickford.

My father knew everyone in the parish and everyone knew my father. Even after I was ordained I was identified as Bill Harris' boy. A death in the parish was a very personal thing: the church was filled at a funeral, and after the return from the cemetery the ladies of the parish served dinner for the family and relatives and anyone else. There were ice-cream socials and chicken dinners and card parties and bingo that brought the parish together as a large family.

The pastor—the old German one—made no bones about public admonitions from the pulpit. My poor uncle who was a butcher and worked late Saturday nights would regularly fall asleep during the sermon and my aunt would be mortified to hear, "And there is Leo P............, sound asleep, when what is being said is particularly good for him to hear." The pastor knew everybody and if you missed church two Sundays in a row, he paid you a visit. When the Depression came, I learned later, he spent every cent of his salary on families in the parish. It was a disgrace to be on relief in those days, but he found a way of helping those who were too sensitive to make their needs known.

Another pastor replaced the German

pastor who was sick and he always ate peanuts when he heard confessions—to keep awake, he told me when I was a priest. We kids went to confession every week whether we needed it or not. And we used to sit on the church steps afterwards until there was a lull. We knew Father would come out and share his peanuts with us.

Church, school, family—these were the environment and these were the dominant influences. It was a simple life and one in which the formative factors were easily controlled. It was a community in which everyone knew everyone else.

Now I am not treating you to a section of my autobiography, but simply pointing out how different our world is now and how many more influences there are in the environment over which we have little control. Those influences are too frequently non-Christian.

The world in which I grew up—rural America—is different from our world today. We can't turn the clock back. But in that world were elements, essential to community, which we have lost. We need to think about that and to dream and plan new forms of Christian community that meet our needs. A wise man said: He who ignores the lessons of history is bound to repeat its mistakes.

There are a number of experiments in

community, both Christian and non-Christian, developing now because there is a growing awareness that lack of community is causing a great deal of personal damage. Groups are living together on farms and ranches, and having as little to do as possible with the rest of society, for they do not share its values. That dropout complex is not the kind of solution a Christian can opt for, for the Christian is to be the salt of the earth, and the potatoes will remain forever unsalted if the salt remains in the container.

I see the fundamental task of the priest today as the creation of the Christian community, for without the community the priest has no function. "He is taken from among men and *ordained for men* in the things that pertain to God," as the Letter to the Hebrews says.

Everything that makes a priest exists because there is a community to be built or supported. His commitment, specifically as a priest, is total commitment to the service of the Christian community. Through Baptism he brings people into the Christian community; through the sacraments of Reconciliation and the Anointing of the Sick he makes the community whole; through the celebration of the Eucharist he deepens the bonds of unity with Christ Jesus and with each other. The word he addresses to the community has

always, as its ultimate purpose, "that they may be one." He is called "Father" because he brings the Christian community into being, not in his own name, but as the instrument of Jesus Christ.

Today modern Christians and modern Christian churches tend to live their lives individualistically. Modern religion is pretty much an affair of me and God, and modern society won't bother you if you keep your religion to yourself.

One of the implications of community is a "stable pattern of interaction" among human beings. That pattern of interaction must support values and for a Christian community that means the teachings of Jesus Christ. The pattern of our society tends to be secular and dehumanizing. The mobility of the society keeps stable relationships from forming. And the pervasiveness of the communications media tends to make the lowest common denominator in values the tone of the environment. About the only thing that can be said for the lowest common denominator is that it is the lowest.

In many places we do not have much experience of the local church as a community. We come together once a week to hear God's word explained in a 10- to 15-minute homily. In so short a time you can't explain much. There is no opportunity for me to say what that means in daily living, how I have lived it, whether this is an insight I never had before and need further understanding about. Now if Christianity is life and not mere teaching, living is more important than hearing.

We come together to celebrate the Eucharist. Eucharist means thanksgiving and celebration means joy. We are gathered about a table because this is a family meal. We are thanking the Father for that great redeeming action of Jesus that broke down the barriers and enabled him to call us brothers. Our hearts are filled with joy because we are Christian brothers and sisters who share one life, one love, one Lord. And we don't even know one another.

About the only time we pray together, outside of Mass, is to recite the rosary at a wake. But there are no moments when we share our prayer, when my prayer pours out from the depths of my heart, depths of sadness or depths of joy, and becomes your prayer. We don't share our prayer, as Jesus did with those close to him. "Holy Father, keep them in your name whom you have given me, that they may be one, even as we are one. . . . I have made known to them your name, that the love with which you have loved me may be in them, and I in them . . . that they may be one in us."

We have prayed together from time to time, but we have never yet prayed like this—"Father, keep Bill in your name, the friend you have given me. May we be one, even as you and Jesus are one . . . may the love with which you have loved Jesus be in him and in me, may Jesus be in him and me, that we may be one in you."

When we put the prayer of Jesus in an immediate human context we see how far our prayer is from his openness. There is power in that kind of prayer: I have manifested your name (all that you are) to the men whom you gave me. When we pray together like that, the Father makes himself known to us and what he is calling us to.

If we are Christians and a Christian community because what we have in common is Jesus Christ as Lord, then it certainly seems that we should be sharing Jesus Christ. Something seems not quite right in the coldness and formalism of our relationship to Jesus Christ and to one another. This sense of uneasiness has suggested a closer look at the early Church. When all else fails read the directions. For quite a while it has been thought that the apostolic and early Church was a particular realization of a certain time and culture. Today a number of people think that the churches at Corinth, Ephesus, Colossae, Philippi, the churches of the Acts of the Apostles are not altogether accidental realizations.

Acts 2:42-47 may be saying something very intrinsic to that word of Jesus, "Love one another as I have loved you." Romans 12:3-21 may be a very immediate application of those words of Jesus, "If I, your Lord and Master, have washed your feet, then you ought to wash one another's feet." The abuses Paul corrects in 1 Corinthians 11:17-14:40 point to an *ideal* of a Christian assembly, and the affectionate salutations with which Paul begins and ends his letters imply close and warm relationships among the saints (Christians).

When we speak about a Christian community we are speaking about creating a Christian environment in which it is easier to be a Christian because there are more Christian influences at work. We are looking at a society which has changed a great deal, and we are asking how does it need to be restructured to sustain the values we want to sustain. It's not a question of turning the clock back. It's a question of dealing with the present moment in an intelligent and creative way. We cannot duplicate the apostolic Church in the 20th century. But we can see elements there that are necessary for any vital realization of the Christian life.

The fundamental pastoral task, as Steve

Clark puts it, "is to build communities which make it possible to live the Christian life." Behind this statement are three fundamental principles:

(1) that a person's beliefs, attitudes, values and behavior patterns (and hence his Christianity) are formed to a great degree by his environment, and, therefore, the normal person needs a Christian environment if he is going to live Christianity in a vital way;

(2) that environmental factors are more basic than institutional factors in Christian growth and, therefore, the primary pastoral concern should be in forming Christian environments rather than in reforming Christian institutions;

(3) that when society as a whole cannot be expected to accept Christianity, it is necessary to form communities within society to make Christian life possible (S. Clark, *Building Christian Communities* p. 23).

If there is one thing community implies it is communion or communication and I strongly suspect that the statement, "I believe in the communion of saints" means "I believe in the communication of Christians." And that requires an act of faith. First, because it isn't very visible, and, secondly, because it is the mystery of God's love working itself out in the openness of Christian brothers and sisters.

There has to be something to communicate about. I would suggest this is the shared experience of conversion to Jesus Christ. We may belong to a Christian institution; we may not belong to Jesus Christ. The function of the institution is to lead us to the personal knowledge and love of Jesus Christ. Many of us have had the experience of being Catholics but not Christians. We have been led to the Church as teacher, but not to Jesus as Lord. When we are centered on Jesus there is a lot to talk about. Often we don't have much to share as Christians because not much is happening as Christians.

Secondly, we need to get to know one another. That does not happen when 700 people gather in one building for an hour a week. The size of a community is not the significant factor. It is the structure. People must be in a stable pattern of interaction. Jesus tells us not to keep our light under a bucket, but we don't share much of anything without knowing one another, including light. That requires contact on a fairly frequent and meaningful level.

All this has implications for the priesthood. The priest must be a leader, that is, he must be able to influence men, to draw them into a oneness of aim and goal and unite them in their approach to that goal. He is not a leader simply because he is a priest. He must

know how to create community and be a part
of it. Too often the priest stands outside the
community, serves it, works on it, but is not a
part of it. And so very often he feels alone.

He needs the support of a community. He
needs a community to pray with. He needs to
know the problems of the community, not
simply hear about them. That will not happen
unless he is part of that community. Perhaps
our pattern of life last year when you and
Bruce and I were living together and praying
together and, at least to some extent, sharing
our lives, is a working model. Our house was
always open, and because it wasn't a rectory
or some other fortified, ecclesiastical place
but simply a house in the community, people
felt easy there—largely because of you and
Bruce—and we were integrated into the life of
the community.

As a leader the priest should see himself
as a catalyst helping others to actualize their
gifts and ministries. He should know how to
associate others with himself in the pastoral
ministry and in other ministries. Some with a
gift of teaching and instruction will prepare
people for Baptism, others will prepare for
Confirmation. Married people could give pre-
marriage instruction much more effectively
than a priest, and might perhaps bring young
people preparing for marriage into their
homes to understand the reality as well as

the romance. A community fund and administrators would develop who generously and tactfully would care for the material needs of the community.

Others would be concerned with the needs of youth, the poor and socially disadvantaged of the neighborhood, the sick, the shut-ins, the elderly. I see the priest as one of a priestly people and his major task is to prepare people to exercise a whole spectrum of ministries that do not require the power of Holy Orders but which have been too long associated with the priesthood of Orders. He will be a man of prayer with his life centered on Jesus Christ. In preparing others to minister he would first of all prepare them to radiate Christ "who has qualified us to be ministers of a new covenant, not in a written code but in the Spirit."

I can see you nodding over the length of this letter already. Sometimes I do get carried away.

May your love abound more and more, with knowledge and all discernment . . . so that you may be pure and blameless for the day of Christ.

**In His love,**
**C.W.H.**

# 5 For the Sake of the Kingdom

*"I do not think a life of celibacy is more difficult than married life. Each day means struggle if it is to mean growth and openness to love. . . . It is always difficult for our self-centeredness to be continually for the other."*

Dear Bill,

One evening last spring when we were enjoying the Chivas Regal Jim had brought, we talked about celibacy and the priesthood. You said that celibacy wasn't a hang-up for you. We drifted on to something else—it was likely the physics midterm you were facing. However, I want to share some further thoughts about it. Celibacy has to be thought through when thinking about the priesthood.

I don't want to imply any lack of appreciation for marriage. Neither of us would exist, nor be what we are, had it not been for those two unique people who lived selfless lives for each of us.

I recall an incident in the life of Pius X—
I believe he himself related it. He had just
been made bishop and the people of his
village had given him a beautiful ring. Sitting
alone with his mother that evening he held it
out to her and said, "Mother isn't it a
beautiful ring? Those people are so good."
She looked down at the simple, gold ring on
her finger whose wornness recalled the hard
years of their peasant life and replied, "Yes,
son, it is very beautiful—but never forget
that if it wasn't for this ring you would never
have had that one."

Well, about celibacy. I know that the lives
of priests sometimes seem cold and
forbidding. I remember that you wrote last
summer that you found it difficult to associate
friendship with being a priest. You wrote,
"One of the ideas that I have . . . is the
connection between priest and condemna-
tion. When did we ever get to see a priest?
(1) in the confessional; (2) at Mass on
Sundays with those sermons; (3) at school
when they came to correct us for something
we'd done wrong."

That made me realize that something
about me as a priest still effectively
concealed the real friendship and love I had
for you, and perhaps the real friendship and
love that can exist in the life of a priest.

Much of current thinking about love is in

terms of romantic love and married love and so we come to take for granted that a celibate life is a loveless life. That is roughly equivalent to saying that it is an inhuman life. Perhaps many of us priests also think of love only romantically, and since we understand that we have given that up, we tend to exclude all love and all warmth from our lives. I don't mean that among priests there have not been friendships—strong, enduring and not very expressive. We knew that in a really tough situation there was someone to whom we could say "help" and it would come. Perhaps over a drink we might have shared a bit of ourselves, but not much. We never prayed together and if I had said to a fellow priest, "Jack, I love you," he would have thought I was both drunk and horny.

Father Powell faced the issue very squarely when he wrote *Why Am I Afraid to Love?* I don't think there was a total lack of love in our lives. It's just that it was so over-spiritualized that it wasn't very often evident.

Don't get me wrong. I think the essence of love is my commitment to your good, as the essence of a human being is rationality. But we don't go around thinking of our friends as rational—we hope they are. We think of them much more concretely, in terms of the beer they like, the old jacket they wear, the way they say "pitcher" for "picture."

So, too, we think of love in the many concrete ways it is manifested and shared. There are no pure essences, as Plato thought. They are all fleshed out in the accidents and happenings of daily living. Love is not a disembodied spirit, although sometimes we try to make it that under the illusion that we thereby keep it pure when the only thing we may be doing is keeping it weak. Real love can be very warm, very affectionate, very expressive, and its strength is its overriding commitment to you.

As I suggested in a previous letter, the natural qualifications for the priesthood are similar to those for marriage. Let me put it a little stronger: the person who is qualified for celibacy is the person who is overqualified for marriage. By this I mean that it is the person who is capable of warm and affectionate relationships who is best qualified for the celibate life. The reason I say this is (1) the celibate life might become a cop-out from relating, and (2) the person who finds warm relationships difficult might find this weakness removed in the intimacy of marriage. For the more one can express a relationship, the deeper it becomes. Certainly marriage offers more ways of expressing a relationship than the celibate life does.

Celibacy is definitely a convenience in the apostolate. It is convenient not to have to worry about supporting a wife and children and to be free to give oneself to the service of the poor and destitute. It is convenient to be able to give every evening to the service of others and not be concerned about neglecting one's family; it is convenient to be able to go at any time to the aid of others without abandoning a responsibility. Some people do choose celibacy because of its convenience, just as some people choose marriage because of its convenience. But fundamentally celibacy, as marriage, is a matter of love.

This is hard for a civilization to understand that understands only romantic love, that does not understand there is a love of friendship that is much more basic in the order of love than romantic love. Aristotle would have understood this; Cicero would have understood this; David would have understood this; those who left wife and children for Jesus' sake would have understood this.

The New Testament tells us that celibacy is chosen for the sake of the kingdom. The kingdom is not of much value. It is the king and relationship with him that is, and Jesus rebuked James and John for concentrating more on the kingdom than on the king. The fundamental reason for the choice of celibacy is for a deeper, more intimate relationship with the Lord.

Celibacy is convenient; it has a witness value—every Christian community should have celibate people. But one chooses celibacy as one chooses marriage—from love. That is the point Paul makes in First Corinthians, too, when he talks about the divided heart. I accept that Paul's advice is qualified by the expression, "because of the difficulty of the times." But Paul is also giving down-to-earth practical advice, as he so often does. He is not developing a theological treatise about a theoretical ideal. No Christian should have a divided heart. But it is very difficult in the guy/girl or husband/wife relationship not to have one.

I know you have experienced this in your relationship with Ann. You know how difficult it has been to keep the Lord first. I think that is a very difficult thing in marriage, too, especially at first, if one has not had a very strong and mature relationship with the Lord beforehand. As married love grows and matures, the Lord comes to have the first and irremovable place, and that is reinforced by the fact that eventually both are centered on the Lord and reinforce that attitude in each other.

But I know cases in which either husband or wife has been profoundly jealous because one loved the Lord more than the partner. Sometimes the center in marriage never gets transferred to the center that can draw both together; gradually the reasons for loving each other grow dim and there is no source of light that can rekindle the vision. Marriage is no guarantee either of intimacy or of love. Both can fail and frequently do when a couple decides to live totally for each other rather than totally for the Lord in each other.

Paul says celibacy removes a very practical difficulty and a very real one. It also creates the *possibility* of a deeper intimacy with the Lord and Paul puts his finger on that. "The unmarried man is anxious about the affairs of the Lord, how to please the Lord; but the married man is anxious about worldly affairs, how to please his wife, and his interests are divided." The ordinary situation is that a friendship grows in proportion to the time and care extended in developing it. Time must be spent together if a marriage is to be successful. The time that a man spends with his wife is time that the celibate is free to spend with the Lord. This suggests a very direct correlation between celibacy for the kingdom and prayer. I want to say something about that later.

Often the celibate life seems a lonely one and to some extent that is true. Loneliness does not, however, rise from a single source, nor does it have a single solution. The awareness of separation from God, for

instance, manifests itself as a deep, psychological loneliness. The awareness of separation is a subconscious awareness of sin and cries out for redemption.

A second source of loneliness is our dependence and insufficiency. We have no control over our human life—we cannot add to it a single day—and we feel isolated and alone. We are aware that our growth and development depend on others. We must open out to love and to be loved, and we cannot do that without others. Thirdly, we are of ourselves inadequate to continue the human race.

Every biological species has a thrust to preserve the species. That biological thrust breaks into our consciousness as the desire or longing to be father or mother. That implies a desire to give, to share, to love, and we experience in ourselves the words of Genesis, "It is not good for man to be alone." It is only this third kind of aloneness that marriage will remove in that intimacy that the bible describes as "being two in one flesh."

But being one in bed and board does not necessarily imply being one in mind and heart. I have seen as great—or even greater —loneliness in married people as I have in celibate people. Every human being needs to love, to be loved, to know the intimacy of profound sharing. That is necessary for the development of the personality.

But it is false to think that this fulfillment can be attained only in marriage. That's one possibility. Jesus needed to be loved, Jesus needed to love. He needed to share and to be supported and he experienced the dreadful loneliness of a man whose friends refused to watch with him. Jesus was a fully developed person. He was not married.

"For human beings, the more powerful need is not for sex per se but for relation-ships, intimacy, acceptance, and affirmation" (Rollo May, *Love and Will,* p. 311).

In a discussion on celibacy the wife of one of my closest friends once remarked, "The reason you priests do not understand celibacy is because you do not understand marriage." I intuitively grasped at once what she meant, although it is hard to put into words and I shall probably do it very badly.

There is a unique kind of love in marriage that seems by its nature to extend only to one and is to last "until death do us part." My mother died when she was 60 and my father remarried a very wonderful and devoted woman who greatly enriched his life. He deeply appreciated and loved her, but he said to me once, "Son, the second marriage is nothing like the first." I understood what he was implying: you can give your heart with that kind of totality only once.

Even among those peoples where polygamy is an institution and the number of wives an index of prestige and influence, there seems always to be a number-one wife. I think this kind of unique, totally giving love is what celibacy for the kingdom means.

Theologians recognize that this kind of celibacy is never temporary. It is always forever. Unless it is this total, it lacks the generosity that makes it an adequate expression of this kind of love, just as people really in love do not take each other for better or for worse until three months elapse. It is until death do us part. The language of love is always forever.

In his *Letters from Prison,* Bonhoeffer remarked, "The essence of chastity is not the suppression of lust but the total orientation of one's life to another." In celibacy that "another" is spelled with a capital "A."

As I said, Bill, I do not in any way want to underestimate marriage in the endeavor to make celibacy understood. I seem to note that esteem for both goes hand in hand. Some Christians are called to marriage that by their mutual love they may help each other grow and increase in the love of God. Others God invites—it is an invitation or a gift—to take a more immediate and direct way: to give to him immediately that total and unique love we can only share with one other. I don't think this happens in a transport of enthusiasm.

There is no "falling in love" with celibacy. There is a gentle drawing to a unique, total and singular relationship with the Lord Jesus. Its essence is commitment and faithfulness, which is the essence of an ideal, lifelong marriage. It's something one renews doggedly every day. It is a gift. It is something received as well as given. Its ultimate purpose, like that of marriage, is realized when Jesus is all in all.

Sure, like you, I have found my heart reaching out for another with the desire to share everything in me; sure, my body yearns in the night for another with whom to share the pulse of life. My arms thrash about and there is no warm nakedness I can enfold. But I know I can't be all things to all men if I am so much for one. Those moments of frustration remind me of an investment I have made —"Where your treasure is, there is your heart also."

Because celibacy is for the kingdom of God—to open our hearts completely to the love of the Lord Jesus, it is clearly not lived alone. John asks, "How can we love the God we do not see, if we do not love the brother whom we see?" But the converse irresistibly follows. If we love the God whom we do not see, must we not love the brother whom we see? The two go together. Ordinarily we grow in this singleness of heart only within the framework of a warm and loving Christian community. Friendships are essential to those who do not have the vocation of a hermit. They offer the intimacy, acceptance and affirmation each of us needs and they relieve the loneliness we would otherwise experience.

Friendship is one of those words whose meaning has been largely eroded by overuse. In philosophy there is a principle that the greater the extension the less the content, or a word that applies to everything means nothing. Friendship is a word that, by a trick of salesmanship, is applied to almost every relationship not overtly hostile. The great classical meaning of the word has been lost, although there are indications that its value as a particular kind of relationship is being rediscovered.

Cicero says, "All I can do is to urge you to put friendship above all other human concerns." For him "friendship is a complete understanding on all things human and divine joined with affection and commitment to the good of each other." Again, "What can be more delightful than to have someone to whom you can say everything with the same absolute confidence as to yourself?"

Father Rene Voillaume: "It is good that a brother knows all that we are and in return shares the same confidence with us. Such a friendship is a great strength. One should be faithful to it. The more a friendship is rooted in depth in the life of the Spirit the more it demands faithfulness."

And David:

I grieve for you, Jonathan, my brother,
dear and delightful you were to me;
your love for me was wonderful
surpassing the love of women.

I would suggest that much of the loneliness that is experienced by the celibate has its sources in a lack of true friendship. I would also suggest that that is the source of much loneliness in marriage. As a recent popular song puts it:

When you gain a lover you lose a friend
The end is the beginning and the beginning is the end.

There has grown up a fear of friendship as a manifestation of latent homosexuality, thanks to Freudian concepts understood and misunderstood. Perhaps that is why we, as men, and as priests, do not form great friendships. Fortunately, there is a growing realization that not all Freud's great insights were infallible and some were downright erroneous. "American men are especially afraid of male friendship lest it have in it some trace of homosexuality" (Rollo May, *ibid,* p. 319).

May also observes, "There are four kinds of love in Western tradition. One is sex, or what we call lust, libido. The second is eros, the drive of love to procreate or create. A third is philia, or friendship . . . the fourth is agape, the love which is devoted to the welfare of the other, the prototype of which is the love of God for man. Every human experience of authentic love is a blending, in varying proportions, of these four. . . . It is only in the contemporary age when we have succeeded, on a fairly broad scale, in singling out sex for our chief concern and have required it to carry the weight of all four forms of love."

Perhaps the most fundamental form of love is friendship. I say fundamental, not in the sense of being that which is first experienced or the most spontaneous. On the contrary, friendship requires a certain maturity, a real love and acceptance of oneself that is a fruit of maturity and that is indispensable for the kind of total openness friendship demands.

Friendship is the basis of our relationship with Jesus—"I have called you friends because I have shared everything with you." Sometimes there is no real friendship with the Lord because there has been no experience of a real friendship with anyone. Perhaps the greatest barrier to developing friendship is not so much the latent fear of homosexuality as the fear of openness and intimacy.

Basically, sexuality is a way of relating to people. "The ideal and normal adult would be one who fully, spontaneously and positively felt the need not only of others, but to be with others and to be something to others" (Don Goergen, *The Sexual Celibate*).

"Every affective relationship involves some sexuality. Although friendships are not best described in sexual terms, they involve the totality of our person. There is more to friendship than our sexuality but we cannot deny that sexuality enters into our friendship" (Erik Erikson, *Identity: Youth and Crisis*).

Strong love of a purely spiritual order is very difficult to have. It is bound to be accompanied by some emotion, by tenderness, by a desire to express that tenderness. The expression of feeling or emotion is no indication of a lack of masculinity. Rather the more comfortable I am with my masculinity the greater freedom, apart from the inhibiting influence of convention, I will have in expression. "When men and women recognize that free expression of affection is certainly nothing to fear, nor a barometer of weakness or effeminacy, all their human relationships, including the sexual one, will be much fuller."

One of the first means of communication in animals and human beings is touch. Because our sensitivity to touch pervades our whole being—only one part of the body sees, only one part hears—it is not only the first but the most available medium of communication.

The newborn baby experiences the love and concern of the mother largely through touch. She kisses and caresses and hugs the baby into a sense of security, a sense of being cared for, a sense of being loved. And so perhaps the most spontaneous expression of affection is the sense of touch. If someone is distressed we instinctively put a hand on his shoulder or take her into our arms. If we love someone very much we reach out to touch or to embrace.

Society is much more permissive of tenderness in a woman than in a man and so she is much more spontaneous and less inhibited in expressing her affection. Society expects strength of a man and so he grows up less expressive of his emotions; emotion is equated with weakness. Emotion is not a weakness. It's a tremendous human quality. If a man wants to throw his arm around his friend and give him a great hug to express what is in his heart, he should.

I shall not develop any thoughts about friendships with women now. You have had some experience of these in high school and I know they have been part of your college life, and not only friendships but romantic relationships as well. Perhaps one views celibacy as putting friendships with women aside. That may be the immediate import of the decision. But friendships with women are important in the life of a priest. They have been important in the lives of the saints. From my own experience I would say it is better to develop these after one has developed mature friendships with men and become mature in developing friendships. We will then know how to be friends without becoming lovers.

As you think about marriage or priesthood and celibacy the important thing to keep in mind is: What is the Lord calling you to? He himself says, "Each has his proper gift, and it is in faithfulness to that gift that we find our fulfillment." I do not think a life of celibacy is more difficult than married life. Each day means struggle if it is to mean growth and openness to love. There is no loving without pain. It is always difficult for our self-centeredness to be continually for the other.

This last has been heavy going, I know. Perhaps I should remind you of the locker room cliche: When the going gets tough, the tough get going. I wish I could have said these things in person so I could know when you were puzzled.

Steve and I went to Ashland yesterday: *Measure for Measure* and *The Rivals* were just first-class theatre. I know you and Ann would enjoy Mrs. Malaprop and her comparisons, such as "as obstinate as an allegory on the banks of the Nile." Why don't you come down? Are you getting any tennis in?

I have missed seeing you this summer. In Paul's words, "God knows how much I long, with the deepest Christian love and affection, for your companionship."

**In His love,
C.W.H.**

P.S. As you think about your decision perhaps one further question would help. Would you become a priest only if you could be a married priest, *i.e.*, supposing that the present discipline of the Church would change so that it would be possible to have a married priesthood?

If your answer is "Yes," that is, if your decision about the priesthood were determined by whether or not priests could marry, then I think you would still have some hard thinking to do on the subject.

# 6 He Went Off Alone to Pray

*"Being faithful in prayer is a real condition of knowing. To me it seems unreal to think we can spend only five minutes with the Lord and expect he will reveal our life's blueprint."*

Dear Bill,

Tom arrived yesterday and the weatherman obligingly turned the thermostat up to the upper 90's just to give him a warm welcome. Last night around eleven we decided to go for a swim in the Rogue. It was just too warm to sleep. The river is low but Father Joe knew a hole and there was enough moon to see where the rocks jutted out. We sat on the rocks afterwards and talked. I told Tom of the letters I was writing to you. He has more than a casual interest after his first year of theology and wants to see them. Maybe you would xerox a copy for him if you still have them about.

I ended my last letter with the thought that our vocations may differ. That is not too important and it is utter nonsense to debate which is the more perfect way of going to the Father. There is only one perfect way and that is the unique way in which he is calling each of us. I admit that I have hoped the Lord was calling you to be a priest, ever since you first talked about it, a year ago. Friends want to share as much as possible. Besides, as our friendship has grown, the qualities I would like to see in a priest, I have discovered in you.

But I have never even prayed that the Lord would call you to the priesthood, only that he would make clear to you what he was calling you to. I guess the reason I never prayed for that was not because I didn't want it, but because I didn't want my desires to influence your decision. I wanted with all my heart that you follow the desire of the Lord for you. That is why I found real encouragement when your prayer life was a regular thing and why I was concerned when it wasn't. As long as we are faithful to prayer we will know what the Lord wants of us.

Being faithful in prayer is a real condition of knowing. To me it seems unreal to think we can spend only five minutes with the Lord and expect he will reveal our life's blueprint. When the Lord calls us to something he prepares us for that. If you read the Gospel of John, you discover that when Jesus said to Peter and Andrew, "Come, follow me and I will make you fishers of men," it was not their first meeting. They had spent some time with him, letting him form their hearts, before that eventful day when he said, "Come." I don't think Jesus acts differently with us. We have to spend time with him, share our lives with him, as friend with friend.

People will not ask anything important of us on our first meeting, if they ask anything at all. Only as we grow together, only as we come to understand one another so well that we know one another's thoughts and anticipate unspoken desires, do we really feel free to ask for something that involves a major commitment. Jesus had to reproach his apostles for that lack of freedom, "Hitherto you have not asked anything in my name," he said. They were hesitant. They had not yet moved from being disciples to being friends, to that sense of total acceptance that set them free to ask for anything. And it was only after Jesus had shared all that he was that he asked them for that major commitment to him which was also a major commitment to one another: "Love one another as I have loved you."

So, too, with us. Until a real closeness has developed between you and Jesus, he will not make known to you what he wants of you. And, secondly, he will not make known to you what he wants of you until your heart is ready to give him whatever he may ask of you. You see, until we can give Jesus what he asks he will not ordinarily ask. He would be putting us in the position of being asked for what we cannot give and no friend would do that.

We can hold no priority above what Jesus wants for us when we come to ask him to reveal his will. That would be phony. It's like saying, "Lord, let me know your will if it is lined up with mine." And in that situation if a guy is really honest, he has to ask, "Who's Lord around here—Jesus or me?" And he has to answer "me." Praying to know God's will implies a kind of openness before the Lord that we are afraid to have. First, we fear that the Lord may ask us to give up the one thing that we don't want to give up, or we fear that if we surrender that completely to the Lord our lives, henceforth, will be perfectly miserable. Neither of these reservations is unusual.

If we have these reservations, the first thing to do is to face them. Honesty in prayer is basic and I think a lot of prayer doesn't get off the ground because it isn't honest. Shakespeare says in Hamlet:

My words fly up, my thoughts remain
   below
Words without thoughts never to heaven
   go.

The reason our prayers don't fly is
because they are not honest, heart-prayers.
Often we have collected the prayer or the
sentiment from a prayerbook. That doesn't
express what we are or where we are. In
themselves they may be very good prayers.
Only they aren't our prayers. It's sort of like
talking to Ann using Romeo's language:

But, soft, what light through yonder
   window breaks
It is the east, and Ann is the sun.

For sheer beauty I doubt you would come
up with anything like that. But I also doubt
whether you would impress Ann, even after
your course in Shakespeare. And so we
ought not to pray "Lord, to suffer or to die,"
as one of the great saints did, if we get ticked
off by a traffic jam. Better pray, "Lord, let me
be patient with all the stupid people you
permit to drive cars on I-5 at 4:30 p.m."
That's where I am. That's what I need.

Being honest in prayer means being pretty
specific. "Help me, Lord, for I am a sinner,"
is a good prayer all right. Anyone but the
Blessed Virgin can say it. But it's much better
to say, "Lord, you know that girl who sits
next to me in history with the short-short skirt
and who crosses her legs and sort of hikes

the skirt up. Help me to keep my thoughts on history and not on her." That's a real prayer because it deals with a specific need. And it's honest.

Sometimes we don't like to admit, even to the Lord, that our thoughts and desires may be touched with lust. We aren't going to shock Jesus by admitting these things are there. When the leper came to Jesus he didn't say, "Lord, I'm not feeling too well." Probably on that day three-fourths of the people in Galilee could have said the same thing. He held out his running sores and twisted fingers and said, "Lord, if you want to, you can make me clean." He had a specific need; he made a specific prayer.

Or I can pray, "Lord, don't let me go too far when I'm with my girl." That's a lot better than saying, "Help me, Lord, because I'm a sinner," but it's a lot better still to pray, "Lord, keep me from French-kissing with my girlfriend when you know wrong things happen." Now I'm being honest and facing the problem. When we start being honest and facing the problem we may begin to discover that we can't pray a specific prayer. I like French-kissing with my girl-friend. A lot of us pray like the young Augustine, "Lord, make me pure—but not yet." When you can't say a prayer you know you ought to pray, tell your problem to the

Lord: "Lord, help me to pray to keep from prolonged French-kissing with my girlfriend."

Do you know what happens when we pray like that? Either we change or we stop praying. You see, we are letting the Lord get right at us where he can heal us. Jesus gave a powerful lesson on this aspect of prayer in the story of the Pharisee and the Publican (Lk 18:9-15). He made it clear that we can't dazzle God by our virtue but we can touch him by our weakness.

One of the things I have admired about you is your total honesty. It has helped me to grow in this direction. I wanted to share with you what that growth has meant in prayer— being honest with the Lord. But you probably have experienced this already. Jesus said, "For everyone who does evil hates the light and does not come to the light, lest his deed should be exposed" (Jn 3:20). Sometimes we are going to be overtaken by darkness but we don't have to love it and we don't have to remain in it. When we come to Jesus honestly he lights up all the dark places in our heart and all those creepy, crawly things that love the dark shrivel up and die, once we let his light touch them.

As friendship grows we become more open and as we become more open friendship grows. Jesus says, "I call you my friends because I have shared everything with you."

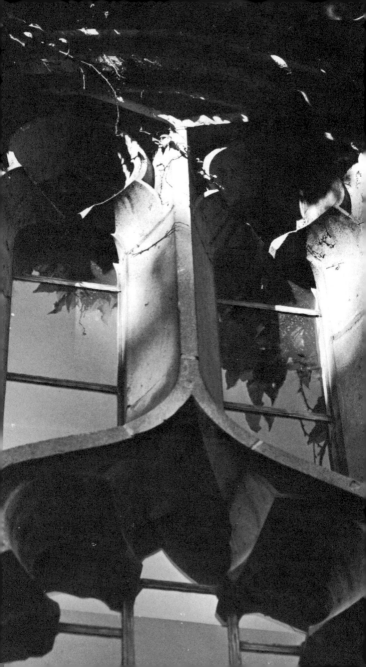

I have found that what has deepened my friendship most with Jesus is being open with him, as it has deepened my friendship with you. The result is that I have been more open to Jesus, and so he has been teaching me more and more about himself.

I know he will never ask anything of us that would make us miserable. He didn't come to make us miserable. He came that we might have life more fully. You know, God's will is not distinct from God's love. God's will is really his passionate longing for us to become fully what he has made us to be. Sometimes our ideas about living life more fully are different from his. Sometimes what he asks is hard because he is calling us to growth. That's where the trust of friendship comes in. Real friendship holds nothing back. Jesus says to us, "Ask and you shall receive." We need to be able to say to him, "Lord, you mean so much to me that you can ask for anything."

Growing in prayer requires regularity and fidelity. We need to put aside for the Lord at least 15 minutes each day of prime time. We grow in friendship most during those moments when we are completely with and for our friends. It is the same with Jesus. Prayer is not all talking. A lot of it is listening. We need some time to become quiet. One of my friends put it, "Don't just do something.

Stand there." Take time—just to stand there. As we relax we sort of let our cares and preoccupations drain away, just to be with the Lord.

Prayer isn't something we do. It is something we let the Holy Spirit do in us. We let him create the conviction that we are sons of the Father and if sons, then brothers of Jesus Christ. Paul calls him our older brother. I've always wanted an older brother, someone I could look up to, be close to. You were more lucky than I. Bit by bit, however, the Spirit has been showing me I have an older brother and more and more my prayer life has been developing in this relationship. Jesus is both friend and brother. (Sometimes brothers aren't friends.)

This happens best when we are aware of the humanness of Jesus. St. Teresa, who knew so much about the wisdom of prayer that she has been proclaimed a doctor of the Church, makes a great point of this. She says: "I clearly see . . . that if we are to please God and he is to grant us great favors, it is his will that this should be through his most sacred humanity. . . . When we are busy, or suffering persecutions or trials, when we cannot get enough quiet, and in times of dryness, Christ is our very good friend. We look at him as a man, we see him weak and in trouble, and he is our companion."

The way we touch God is through the humanness of Jesus. That is what mediator means—we can reach something beyond us through something that is with us. Prayer gets unreal when we lose sight of the humanness of Jesus. The New Testament tells us that he "is the visible image of the invisible God."

Everything about God that can be translated into human language is expressed in Jesus. Do you know what happens when we lose contact with the humanness of Jesus? We lose real contact with God. When we translate the humanness of Jesus back into divinity we not only make a bad translation, but we lose the opportunity of any understanding of God at all. We don't know God's language. In the Old Testament he spoke through the prophets but sometimes the message was not clear. That's not surprising. Whenever God uses a human instrument the result is always imperfect. So God decided to send his Son to speak for him. He would get it straight. That's where we get it straight.

Father Capon in his book, *Hunting the Divine Fox,* says we have a tendency to think of Jesus as superman who flips about himself his cloak of invisibility and gets away from tough situations. He writes: "When we imagine him as a child, for example, we somehow feel obliged to say that he was a little freak who never hid when his mother called him [we know that he did at least once —in the Temple], who always put his toys away in his toy box, and who, when he got to the age at which boys have wet dreams, piously refused to have any." You know, a lot of people really flip out when I quote this sentence. Why? Because all of a sudden the real humanness of Jesus has shattered their preconceived image of a superman. Yet the bible says that he took upon himself all our human weaknesses, except sin. As we grow up and come to know sin I suppose that is the weakness that troubles us most. But there are a lot of human weaknesses that are not sin. Maybe that is why children more easily identify with the humanness of Jesus. They know weakness but not sin. This is one of the places where it is easiest to meet Jesus—in our mutual experience of weakness.

One of the places where I have been able to come very close to him is in the garden of Gethsemane. Mark writes:

He took with him Peter, James and John, and began to be horror-stricken and desperately depressed.

"My heart is nearly breaking," he told them. "Stay here and keep watch with me." Then he walked forward a little way and flung himself on the ground, praying that, if it were possible, he might not have to face the ordeal.

Then he came and found them fast asleep. He said to Peter, "Are you asleep, Simon? Couldn't you manage to watch for a single hour?"

Lord, I know your experience. I know those moments of deep discouragement and depression when one really needs the strength and the understanding and the love of a friend. But I never thought you knew them, too. You always seem so cool—and now—your heart is nearly breaking. You had shared everything with those three—Peter, James and John: the overwhelming moment on the mount of the Transfiguration when the glory of heaven enfolded them, that distressful moment when they could no longer handle the boat and you silenced wind and waves, those evenings when you camped out with them on the side of a hill and spoke to them of your love for them around the fire that had cooked their supper, and then stretched out alongside them because you had nowhere else to lay your head.

But now—when you really needed them— they were fast asleep. You needed the strength of their human love before the great demand of your Father; you needed their human closeness, just one of them to put his arm around you and say, "Lord, we're with you" at this moment when you were so down; you needed one of them to share the beat of your troubled heart and let you know you didn't have to go it alone.

Lord, I know those moments when I looked for someone to comfort me and I found none. Someone to help me pray when I was down and I was left alone—with my doubt and confusion and my weakness of faith. And those moments when my heart really ached—moments when I tried to love and was misunderstood, tried to help and was rejected and wanted to share that hurt but was too inhibited to let go. I know now, Lord, that you experienced that, too, when not even your friends understood or cared. I don't know, Lord, whether I can ever share your cross. I'm pretty weak. But I can share your heartbreak for I, too, am often alone.

There are a lot of other human moments in the gospels where we can identify with Jesus and move into the openness of deep friendship. I think I told you how difficult I found it to give in to his request each day to "watch one hour with him." I still struggle to be faithful to that. It's hard, and yet I know I can't be like him if I am not with him. That is one thing he wants of both of us . . . that we be like him . . . and that means we must be with him.

If I were you I would finish up the course and not drop it. There are only three more weeks left. I know classes all year around are a drag, and work with study in the summer especially so. But you can make a B easily and that will save you a whole term.

Ted says you are renewing the face of the farm and appreciates your being a really good worker.

I'll see you at the end of August.

As Paul says, "Let us steadfastly maintain the habit of prayer."

**God's peace!**
**C.W.H.**

# 7 A Man After God's Own Heart

*"Your thoughts about the priesthood were perhaps prompted more by a sense of obligation than of attraction."*

Dear Bill,

As we have written and talked through the summer it has become more and more clear to me that the Lord is not calling you to be a priest. Of that I am 70 percent sure. I've prayed and fasted about it since June, asking the Lord to make your decision clear by September. It was your final willingness to let go, to give up Ann—if that was what the Lord was asking—that gave the right perspective. Once the Lord is in first place what he wants grows clear, and is confirmed by that inner peace only he can give.

I also think he is saying, "Wait"—there is still a work he wants to do in you. I would suggest that you really wait upon him until he says, "Now is the acceptable time."

Your thoughts about the priesthood were perhaps prompted more by a sense of obligation than of attraction. Many of us have grown up with the assumption that only in the priesthood can one find the fullness of Christian life and the opportunity to serve the Christian community. Since you wanted to be totally the Lord's and to serve his people you felt you had to be a priest (and were afraid of that). The decisive thing for me was in your lack of joy in the thought of being a priest.

I still have the conviction that the Lord is calling you to live intensely for him, to be a man after God's own heart. I know Ann will not discourage that, although she may be puzzled by it. One of Mary's treasured words in the gospel is, "Do whatever he tells you" (Jn 2:5). That is my ongoing prayer with and for you.

Your friendship means much to me and the trust with which you have shared this decision. I hope that as we become more and more firmly grounded in the Lord that friendship will grow in strength and commitment. "So, my brother whom I love and long for, do stand firmly in the Lord, and remember how much I love you."

**In His love,
C.W.H.**